Guyness

Deal with it

body and soul

Steve Pitt • Illustrated by Steven Murray

James Lorimer & Company Ltd., Publishers
Toronto

It's the first day of

school and you go to your dresser to pull out your favourite T-shirt. But wait — there's a note from your sister in the drawer. "Borrowed one," it says. "Feel free to take something of mine!"

Yeah, right. As if you would be caught dead wearing your sister's clothes. It's so unfair. People say all the time that boys and girls are equals, but you can't help noticing a big difference in the way they expect you to act.

Boys are expected to behave differently and have different interests than girls — as if all guys like sports, cars, and computer games. But what if you don't? And what happens when you get upset or hurt yourself? Seems like girls can cry any time they want, but it's not the same for boys.

It can be hard to know exactly what being a guy is all about.

That's because we often treat people differently because of their gender — whether they're male or female, a boy or a girl, a man or a woman. We expect guys to have certain traits and girls to have certain traits. These expectations can cause problems when they are used to judge someone.

Ideas about being a guy are changing all the time.

They can be very different from generation to generation or among different cultures. No matter what you do, there may be times when you feel like you don't fit in.

This book can help you understand where our ideas about guyness come from, how they can create conflict in your life, and how to deal with problems when they arise.

Contents

What is

Hey, everyone knows the difference between guys and girls, right?

Guyness is another word for masculinity. And isn't masculinity about...

- taking risks?
- playing rough and rude?
- not showing weakness?
- liking sports, technology, and outdoor stuff?
- being physically strong?
- doing better in math than in reading?
- not minding getting dirty?
- being a take-charge sort of person?
- being born a guy?

Guyness?

Yeah, we all know guys like that. Some of us are guys like that. But there are also lots of guys who:

- take care of others
- are sensitive
- like cooking and crafts
- enjoy reading
- love long phone conversations
- are graceful and artistic
- like kids and babies
- dress in clean, neat clothes.
- are certain they were born guys, even if others think they are girls

When you think about it, the only thing that all guys have in common is that they're all, well, guys!

Guyness 101

Ideas of guyness can be

based on . . .

QUIZ

Tradition or truth?

Nearly every time we watch a movie, read a book, or even just walk down the street we see stereotypes, or pre-set ideas about what groups of people are like. When stereotypes lead to people being treated differently or being excluded, that's discrimination. Discrimination based on someone's gender is called — you guessed it — gender discrimination. In the following situations, is someone being discriminated against because of their gender? Check out the answers on the opposite page.

 Not Identical
Your twin sister is always being asked to babysit kids in your neighbourhood. You'd like to try babysitting, too, but no one ever asks you.

 Blind about Blondes
Randy is always telling blonde jokes at school. Serena tells him she finds his jokes offensive.

 Women's Work
Your mom asks you to dust the living room. Your father tells you that housework is for girls and says you should be mowing the lawn instead.

 Play Ball!
The all-boys softball team has just been challenged by the champion girls' team to a game. Some of the guys don't want to play against the girls, afraid they might lose.

 Pasta Passion
You love your grandmother's homemade pasta. Grandma has taught all your sisters to make pasta, but she's never asked if you'd like to learn.

 ### School of Rock
Aric loves playing guitar, but his friends tease him because his teacher makes him practise classical music instead of rock.

 ### Brother Bully
Your brother wants you to try something too risky on your bike. You're a good rider, but come on! When you say, "No way!" your brother calls you Chicken Girl.

 ### Just the Girls
Your aunt often takes your sister out for Girls Night Out evenings. She never asks if you want to come along.

 ### Nursery Rhyme
An old rhyme says boys are made of "snips and snails and puppy dog tails," or are born naughty, and girls are made of "sugar and spice and everything nice," or are born nice.

 ### Up in Arms
You and your friends see two guys walking arm-in-arm. One of your friends laughs out loud and starts calling them fags.

Answers

1. No. If someone rejected your offer to babysit because of your gender, that would be discrimination. But it sounds like you haven't made people aware of your interest.

2. Yes. Did you ever notice that blonde jokes are almost always about women and not men? Some people like to tell jokes that make one group of people look stupid. And that's a form of discrimination.

3. Yes. Your dad's comment is based on old ideas about the types of work that men and women are best suited for. Your mother, on the other hand, is not letting stereotypes affect the way your household is run.

4. Yes. A true champion enjoys playing against the best competition, regardless of gender.

5. Yes. But your grandma would likely be thrilled that you want to learn how to make her pasta!

Don't shy away from learning a new skill because of your gender.

6. Yes. The idea that classical music is somehow less masculine than rock music is simply not true.

7. Yes. Boys and girls both need to use common sense.

8. No. Sometimes women and girls — or guys, for that matter — like to bond over things they have in common. Your aunt doesn't mean to exclude you; she just wants some private time with your sister.

9. Yes and no. When old ideas about gender make you see or treat boys and girls differently, that's discrimination.

10. Yes. In many cultures, members of the same sex walk arm-in-arm or holding hands as a sign of friendship. Since your friend clearly assumes that it means they are gay, and that it means there is something wrong with them, he is discriminating against them.

Dear Guyness Counsellor

Q. I have one brother and two sisters. Sometimes it seems like there's a completely different set of rules in our house for the boys and the girls. Like, my brother and I get to stay out later, but my sisters get bigger allowances so they can buy girl stuff like makeup. It's unfair all around!

— Divided

A. It's very common for families to have different rules for guys and girls — but that doesn't make it fair. Call a family meeting to explain your feelings and try to work out some compromises.

Q. My grandpa is a fun old hippie. He loves his garden and refuses to own a car. Last year, someone gave him an old bicycle that he rides everywhere. Trouble is, it's a girl's bike and he looks silly riding it. Every time they see him coming, my friends tease me about my "bearded grandma." Why does he have to be so feminine? — *Embarrassed*

A. The problem isn't that your grandfather seems feminine, or womanly. In fact, it sounds like he's very secure in his masculinity! Men like this are often confident and understand that male stereotypes are just that — stereotypes. Sounds like your grandfather isn't worried that riding a girl's bike makes him less of a man. As with many things in his life, he goes his own way. The real problem here is that you're embarrassed. Instead of feeling ashamed of your grandfather, how about taking his lead and becoming more confident in who you are?

Q. My favourite movie character never shows pain, even when someone drops him from a helicopter or smacks him with a two-by-four. I want to be tough like him. But yesterday I hit my elbow so hard I actually cried! Am I a sissy? — *Feelin' Mo Pain*

A. Remember that movies are not real life. When actors "hit" each other, the punches and kicks don't really connect. Stunt doubles and special effects make it look like the actors are in danger when they're not — that's why it's called acting! Movies are fun to watch, but that doesn't mean it's funny to hit your funny bone. So what if you cried? It hurt, didn't it?

Q. Every guy I see on TV, in magazines, or in movies is super buff. I guess I'm supposed to look like that. What am I doing wrong? — *Noodle Arms*

A. If you found an old Superman or Batman comic from the 1940s, you would see that even superheroes have not always been the muscle freaks you see these days. Somehow, massive muscles have become the current male ideal. But remember, no normal person looks like that. Those actors, models, and athletes work out, eat special diets, and may even take steroids or undergo surgery to look the way they do. Focus on being healthy and not on achieving an unrealistic image of masculinity.

Q. I really like hanging out with my friend Kumar, but when he comes to our house he gets really weird. If my sisters say hello, he looks away and pretends he does not see them. If my mother asks him a question, he ignores her and talks to me as if she is not there. When I asked him about it, he just muttered something about how he doesn't want to be rude. Well, isn't he being rude? — *Kinda Ticked Off*

A. In some cultures, the males of one family are not allowed to talk to or mix with the females from another. Your friend may come from such a culture. You should let him know that in your family it is okay to for him to talk to your mother and sisters as long as he is respectful. If he is not comfortable with that, you two should find somewhere else to hang out. Keep in mind that if you visit Kumar at his house, you will be expected to respect his family's rules.

Myths

All boys like...

Never use generalizations about any group of people. Everyone has special likes and dislikes. The only generalization that's true is that all people are unique in some way.

HOUSEWORK is women's work.

There was a time when most women worked at home, while their husbands held jobs outside of the home. These days, families do things differently. Men are just as qualified as women to do housework.

Guys are not as sensitive as girls.

A boy's feelings can get hurt just as easily as a girl's, but boys are often taught not to show their emotions. Inside, though, are those same hurt feelings.

DID YOU KNOW?

- Pink was once a boy's colour because it was flashy and aggressive.

GUYS
are hard-wired to be
tough.

While some people think that it is a male's "nature" to be aggressive, dominant, and competitive, others argue that parents and teachers raise boys to these stereotypes, or "nurture" these ideas. Whether these traits are based on "nature," "nurture," or some combination, it is unfair to say that having less of them makes a guy unmasculine.

BOYS are
stronger than girls.

Most — but not all — men are physically larger and stronger than women. But studies have proven that women can bear more physical pain than men. And there are other forms of strength that are not related to gender at all.

YOU'RE BOY
if that's what your BIRTH CERTIFICATE says.

A birth certificate describes a person's most basic physical appearance at birth. It cannot predict what kind of personality or gender a person will grow up to have. You're a boy if that's what you say.

- Pants are a recent invention. Many great warriors, from Alexander the Great to Julius Caesar, fought wars in skirts. Elite Scottish and Greek soldiers still wear skirt-like uniforms.

- In the Victorian age, very young children — both girls and boys — wore long hair and dresses.

Ever get tired of hearing "it's a guy thing?"

Sure, some boys like watching sports, playing video games, streaming gory movies, and all that stuff. Not you. But you often go along with what your friends want to do because you're afraid of not fitting in. Cause waves? No way! Or maybe you do like that stuff, but you still feel a lot of pressure to act a certain way — like never letting on when things get to you. Problem is, a lot of things get to you.

Gender stereotypes don't cause problems only for girls. For everyone, not fitting in can lead to feeling:

- embarrassed
- left out
- discouraged
- pressured
- depressed
- jealous or resentful of others
- bullied or teased.

DEAR DR. SHRINK-WRAPPED . . .

Q: There's a girl named Nellie in my class who I'd really like to ask to the school dance. Trouble is, I just found out that she is a national karate champion and I don't want to be "the guy dating a girl who could beat him up."

— *Nervous About Nellie*

A: Dr. Shrink-Wrapped would like to see anyone who disses you for dating this girl get his head examined! Gender stereotypes would have all guys avoiding girls who:

- are physically strong
- have their own opinions
- have competitive spirit
- let their ambitions come before ours
- have control of their emotions.

It's silly to think that these things make a girl more of a man than the guy she is with. Don't let gender stereotypes stop you from doing what you want to do. If you like this girl, you should ask her out. If the other guys make jokes, they're probably jealous that you are dating such an interesting and athletic person. Eventually, they'll lay off.

Q: There are two little kids on my street, and I often watch them when their mother is too busy. But they keep hitting me when we play. I'm twice their size, so I could knock both of them to the moon if I wanted, but my parents have always told me to never get into fights. I mentioned this to their mother, but she just shrugged and said, "Boys will be boys."

— *Black & Blue*

A: Dr. Shrink-Wrapped can see that those little boys are the ones with the problem. Their mother is passing on to them the old stereotype that all guys play rough. Don't you buy it, and don't let them, either. They probably have no idea they are hurting you. You have to tell them that hitting is not acceptable and, if they try it, you will not play with them. Once they realize that you mean it, the hitting should stop.

You might be Black & Blue, but you deserve a pat on the back for being true blue to yourself. You don't believe the silly stereotype that only girls like kids and make good babysitters. These two boys look up to you because you are so much bigger and stronger than they are; let them copy your smarts in knowing that harming people can get you into trouble.

Mr. **Nice Guy**

QUIZ

Are you a good guy?

When dealing with conflict, there are three ways to go. You can be the **fall guy** and shoulder all the responsibility for the situation, you can be a **tough guy** and push others around, or you can be a **good guy** and try to find a compromise that everyone can live with. Take this quiz and check out your behaviour on the next page.

❶ TRUCK TROUBLES

Your friends are going to a monster truck show. You hate that stuff. Do you: a) tell them that only morons would want to watch it? b) go and pretend to like it so they won't tease you? c) firmly tell them you won't go and stand up to their teasing?

❷ *Jock Strapped*

Your uncle Norman is a jock and he keeps sending you sports equipment for your birthday. He knows you hate sports, but he hopes someday you'll change your mind. Every time you open his present, you feel as if you are being criticized. This year he sent you a lacrosse stick. Do you: a) thank him as usual? b) explain to him how his presents make you feel? c) tell him you know a good place where he can stick the lacrosse stick?

❸ Choice Challenge

You have two friends, Rostam and Wayne, with very different interests. You have already agreed to go with Rostam to see the latest action movie on Saturday, but then Wayne says he has free tickets to a rare exhibit of dinosaur fossils at the museum. You would rather see the fossils, but are afraid that Rostam will tease you for being a nerd. Do you: a) tell Rostam your Aunt Millie was struck by a meteor and you have to go to the funeral on Saturday? b) go to the movie with Rostam, and tell him about Wayne's lame idea of going to a museum? c) explain to Rostam that the museum exhibit is a once-in-a-lifetime opportunity and reschedule the movie?

❹ MARTIAL SMARTS

Your dad wants you to take up tae kwon do to develop your "fighter" instinct because he thinks you're too passive. But lessons fall on the same night as your book club. Do you: a) avoid your dad until he forgets all about it? b) go to tae kwon do and try to beat up other kids until your dad leaves you alone? c) suggest to your parents that maybe you could do both as long as the book club has priority?

5 PIE PROBLEM

Your grandmother is teaching you how to make an apple pie. Your friends show up at the door to ask if you want to play baseball. Unfortunately, you forgot that you are wearing an apron and they start laughing at you. Do you: a) threaten that you'll smash their faces if they tell anyone what they saw? b) tear off the apron and tell them that your mother forced you to spend time with Grandma? c) laugh at yourself and invite your friends in for some pie?

6 THE WRONG FOOT

Your favourite rapper, Nasty Dog Ned, wears black shoes with pink laces. You convince your parents to buy you shoes and laces just like Ned's, but when you wear them to school your friends, and even your teachers, make fun of your new sneaks. Do you: a) throw the shoes and laces in the garbage and tell your parents someone stole them? b) laugh along with them? c) yell at your friends and vandalize the classrooms of the teachers who laughed?

7 For Arts Sake

You love art class, and think you might have real talent. You are fascinated by fabric sculpture, but your mom seems reluctant to let you use her sewing machine, saying a boy will be too hard on it. Do you: a) explain to your mom that you will be very careful with her sewing machine, and show her gallery catalogues with prices that fine art pieces can be sold for? b) use the sewing machine behind your mother's back? c) give up on your art and take up football?

8 Florence Nightinguy

When you were in the hospital with a broken leg, one of your nurses was a guy. It got you thinking: you would like to do something to help people, and maybe you should look into a career as a nurse. But your guidance counsellor has said that nursing is for girls. Do you: a) make another appointment with a different counsellor? b) forget it, and try to think of something more manly to do with your life? c) post nasty things about the guidance counsellor on the Internet?

Answers

1. a) Tough Guy	2. a) Fall Guy	3. a) Tough Guy	4. a) Fall Guy	5. a) Tough Guy	6. a) Fall Guy	7. a) Good Guy	8. a) Good Guy
b) Fall Guy	b) Good Guy	b) Fall Guy	b) Tough Guy	b) Fall Guy	b) Good Guy	b) Tough Guy	b) Fall Guy
c) Good Guy	c) Tough Guy	c) Good Guy	c) Good Guy	c) Good Guy	c) Tough Guy	c) Fall Guy	c) Tough Guy

How to be a Good Guy

There are some basic things you can do to make it easier for other guys — and yourself — to be whatever they choose.

Beware of "good" stereotypes. If everyone believes that guys are automatically good at something, what's bad about that? Well, what about the guys who are not good at whatever it is? What about girls who are? All stereotypes generalize, and generalizations don't leave room for individual differences.

Be sensitive. Not "cry every three seconds" sensitive, but aware of how your words and actions affect other people. You might be the smartest, funniest guy in town, but if what you say and do is offending people, soon there will be nobody around to listen.

Stay cool. You might think that you have to react to everything, but if your first reaction is an aggressive one, then stop yourself. Listen to the other person, count to ten, and think before acting.

Learn about guyness from girls. Spend time with them, listen to them, and learn what they think about gender stereotypes. Even if every guy around thinks it's okay for guys to objectify women, you can be sure that less than half the population is convinced.

Remember that ideas about gender can be culturally specific. Behaviour that you consider acceptable for men or women might be frowned upon in another culture, and vice versa. While you want to respect the attitudes held by other people, you can still stand up against gender rules that infringe upon anyone's basic rights.

✓ Do be proud of who you are and how you define guyness for yourself.

✓ Do share your concerns with your parents or an adult you can trust.

✓ Do experiment with how you see guyness.

✓ Do accept others who are different than you.

✓ Do practise standing up for yourself in all situations.

✓ Do question all stereotypes about guys.

✓ Do find ways to try and make your favourite activities interesting to your friends.

✓ Do look around to see if there are other kids who already share your interests.

✓ Do your homework. Go to the library and see if there are books and magazines about the things you like to do.

✓ Do present a positive image of yourself on social media.

✗ Don't change what you do just to please others.

✗ Don't let stereotypes affect the way you value yourself.

✗ Don't let gender expectations limit or change your hopes and dreams.

✗ Don't bottle up your feelings and become angry.

✗ Don't think of your gender as a trap.

✗ Don't put down other people's interests just because they do not appeal to you.

✗ Don't allow people to make you feel bad for liking different things.

✗ Don't be thin-skinned. You can put up with a little harmless teasing.

✗ Don't be afraid to be yourself.

✗ Don't use social media to make others feel bad about how they present themselves.

Learn about guyness from other guys. This doesn't mean you should do everything the way, say, your father does. Look at what you admire in your male role models. Try to incorporate these traits into your own ideas about guyness.

- The ancient Druids sacrificed their first born male child as a bribe to the gods to send more male children.

- In the 18th century, boys as young as five years old served aboard European warships.

The **Wise Guy**

You love being a guy!

All the girls love your tough attitude and other guys admire you. Your coaches say you're a natural leader. You're happy to leave the girl stuff to the girls, and your dad says you're a chip off the old block. Hey, girls and guys are different, and you like it that way. All right, maybe your grades are slipping because you never ask for help. And it bugs you that whenever you say something from the heart, people think you're just kidding around. And, okay, sometimes it would be nice to have a real conversation with a girl — you know, about important stuff — without people thinking you're trying to pick her up or going all soft.

But gender stereotypes don't really affect you.

Or do they?

do's and don'ts

✓ Do question all stereotypes about gender.

✓ Do look past how people look and dress.

✓ Do think about the similarities between boys and girls.

✓ Do look at people as individuals, not just as a member of a gender.

✓ Do think for yourself.

✓ Do choose your words carefully to make sure you're not using hurtful language.

✓ Do try new things.

✓ Do encourage those who are less gifted in some way.

✓ Do hand out compliments. Negative comments are never appreciated.

✓ Do learn to "live and let live."

✗ Don't make assumptions based on gender.

✗ Don't judge people by how they look.

✗ Don't assume adults have no biases.

✗ Don't just believe what others say about someone.

✗ Don't be closed-minded about differences between people.

✗ Don't assume older traditions are better.

✗ Don't see people as just part of a group instead of as individuals.

✗ Don't let old-fashioned gender roles stand in your way of doing what you want to do.

✗ Don't be afraid to look bad when you try something new. You will get better with practise.

QUIZ

Do you take it like a man?

Are you the perfect guy on someone else's terms, or on your own? It's hard to know if you're just being you, or if you're changing your behaviour because of what everyone else thinks a guy should be. Take this quiz and see what you can find out. Of the following statements, how many are true, how many are false?

1. All guys like the same things.

2. I never try to do something I might not be good at.

3. If I try something new and fail, I immediately quit.

4. People should solve their own problems.

5. People judge you solely on your accomplishments.

6. If you show your soft side, people won't respect you.

7. The world is a very competitive place.

8. You'd have to be gay to be interested in things like clothes, grooming, and decorating.

9. The best way to impress a girl is to act cool and aloof.

10. Never show fear.

Girls are way too sensitive about jokes and stupid insults. **11**

Only girls get messed up about food and body image. **12**

Men and women are better suited for different jobs. **13**

All this transgender stuff is lame. If your birth certificate says you're a guy, then you're a guy. **14**

Men make better leaders than women. **15**

Girls need guys to protect them. **16**

Girls need to know a guy is in charge. **17**

Guys are more independent than girls. **18**

It's important to be in total control of yourself at all times. **19**

You can measure a guy's success by how much money he has or by the stuff he owns. **20**

Did you score a lot of Trues? Maybe it's time to think about how you treat people who don't follow the gender rules as you see them, and to talk to someone about how your definition of guyness might be limiting you.

The **Wise Guy**

There are some simple things you can do **to protect yourself from gender discrimination.**

Have confidence in yourself
People are often afraid to be different from their friends because they think they will get teased. But think about the coolest people you know — they are admired for going their own way. Remember, every new idea or trend started with one person who wasn't afraid to be different.

Make a joke
Humour is a great way to defuse confrontation. If you can make a joke that doesn't put you or the other guys down, your shared laughter can turn the focus away from you as a victim of their teasing. You might find that they come to appreciate your sense of humour and respect you despite your differences.

Do some research
There are probably famous people who share the same interests that you do, or have faced the same obstacles that stand in your way. You may never get to meet these folks, but somehow the world feels a little less lonely if you find out that you can identify with someone successful.

Talk to an older guy
Do you think you are the first person in the world to feel lonely and misunderstood? Everyone feels this way at some time or another. Often the best way to learn about being a guy is to talk to someone who has more experience than you. A big brother, father, or even your grandfather may have answers to your questions about guyness.

DID YOU KNOW?

- Male professional speed swimmers shave their legs and chests to reduce water resistance.

When the Media is Involved

It isn't just family, friends, and teachers who send us messages about guyness. The media also plays a part. Think of how much time you spend watching movies or TV, playing video games, listening to music, and reading books or magazines. What if all these things are sending you messages about masculinity that are outdated, unfair, or just plain wrong?

The people who create the media aren't concerned about what's best for you when they show an image of a guy. They might be trying to sell products, attract advertisers, or make something as exciting and sexy as possible so people will like it. As a result, the media often portrays guys in stereotypical ways, and has even invented new stereotypes. Here are some things the media tells us about guys:

- Violence is natural for guys.
- A guy has to drink hard and play hard.
- Guys have to be muscled and strong to be attractive.
- The ability to dominate other people is the most important thing about a guy.
- For a guy to be successful, he has to be more ruthless than the competition.
- Girls will be interested in you if you buy the right things.

The other thing the media does is try to tell us that it's okay for girls and women to be treated like they are objects just for the pleasure of guys. This objectification of women is offensive — and what does it say about men? Consider this: do you really think your worth as a human being relies on how many rights you take away from other people?

So, what can you do about this? Break down how much time and money you spend on the media, and compare this with what you think is really important in your life.

- Cut back on your intake of influences like violent video games, movies, or shows.
- Increase your time reading books, especially those that contain complex images of guys.
- Start discussing what you see on social media with family and friends.
- Avoid media that objectify women, such as certain online videos or video games.
- Question everything you see or read, especially in advertising and on social media.
- Remember that images of male celebrities in all sorts of media are often illusions.

Challenge stereotypes
Our society is still full of old-fashioned ideas of what guys are supposed to be like and what they are supposed to do. If you want to do something and someone says "But guys don't do that," you should ask why. If they cannot provide a good answer, you should do what you want.

- Male Emperor Penguins guard the nest and eggs for up to 65 days waiting for their mates to return with food.

- Male seahorses carry developing seahorses in their bodies until their babies are ready to be born.

Have you ever seen another guy having trouble because of ideas about guyness?

Was he getting picked on? Did you stand up for him? Do anything?

Well, why not?

The Power of Silence

It's scary to speak up when you don't like what you see around you. You worry about the consequences of standing up for your own ideas of guyness. You might get teased, lose friends, get told off, or cause someone to get into trouble. But when you say nothing, it's almost like you're saying, "It's okay. What you're doing is fine by me."

Start the Change

Speaking up when you've been a witness to gender discrimination is hard work. You may feel like what you have to say is not important and won't do anything. But change can start with one person. And that person could be you!

do's and don'ts

✓ Do speak your mind if you feel safe enough to do so.

✓ Do tell a trustworthy adult about what you've witnessed.

✓ Do offer support and friendship to the target.

✓ Do keep an open mind about what guyness means.

✓ Do support those around you who are different.

✓ Do feel you have a voice and an ability to affect the world around you.

✓ Do talk to your friends when you see them displaying gender discrimination.

✓ Do remember that you are important to your friends.

✓ Do make sure the discussion stays civil.

✓ Do your own thing if need be.

✓ Do remember that your concept of guyness has to include how you treat girls and women.

✗ Don't change your behaviour to get along better with others.

✗ Don't use sexist language.

✗ Don't stay silent.

✗ Don't encourage the mocking of others by laughing or spreading gossip.

✗ Don't allow yourself to be bullied into supporting one of your friends.

✗ Don't be surprised if being reasonable is sometimes perceived as being weak.

✗ Don't be afraid to speak up for yourself.

✗ Don't hold a grudge.

✗ Don't let friends get away with bad manners.

✗ Don't ignore ideas of girlness; they are part of your own definition of guyness.

The **Witness**

QUIZ

Do you really get it?

Being a guy is complicated. Sometimes you see things happen that you think are not right. Take this quiz to see how you'd react as a witness to gender stereotypes and discrimination. This quiz has no right or wrong answers, because each situation is unique. Your answers may be different from the ones given below, but they could be right under the circumstances.

① CHORE BORE

Two girls have joined your Scout troop. When you went camping, the girls were assigned the unpleasant camp chores, such as fetching water and scrubbing pots. You know that this is what happens to all junior Scouts, but the girls think they are being picked on because they are female.

- See if things can be changed so that chores are shared more equally.
- Suggest to your troop leader that there be a group meeting where these traditions and rules are laid out.
- Let the girls know that all the new scouts get the worst chores.

② FAVOURITE FERRET

Every weekend, someone gets to take Stinky the ferret home from school. That privilege goes to whoever has the neatest desk that week. The trouble is, only the girls ever seem to win. Many of the boys in your class have even given up trying to win Stinky.

- Make an effort to keep your desk neat, and see if the teacher still chooses a girl.
- Point out to the teacher that the boys never win, and ask if the rules can be changed.
- Have a class discussion on making a schedule for taking Stinky home so everyone gets the chance the same number of times.

3 Cry "Uncle"

Your uncle Arnold is always calling your little brother Little Girly Man because he cries when he is angry. You know Uncle Arnold is just kidding, but you also know that calling your little brother names just makes him cry more.

- Explain to Uncle Arnold that name-calling won't change your brother's behaviour.
- Make it a joke with your brother and make up silly, non-hurtful names for everyone in the family.
- Tell your parents that Uncle Arnold's behaviour is making your brother ashamed of showing his feelings.

4 B-Ball Blues

One of your teammates is a terrible basketball player, but he has fun playing. His mother looks for excuses for why her son is so lousy. She says it's the coach's fault, or yells nasty things at her son's teammates, including you. Your friend is humiliated, the coach is talking about cutting him from the team, and the fun of playing is disappearing.

- Have a talk with your teammate about how his mother's assumptions about all guys being good at sports are hurting him.
- Go with your friend to talk to the coach about playing just for fun.
- Suggest your teammate talk to his mother about gender stereotypes.
- Have a team meeting to discuss rules for parents' behaviour at games.

5 Gang "Bang!"

Your little brother loves movies and TV shows that promote the stereotype of tough, violent men as role models. They have the right to take what they want, no matter who gets hurt. And they in return they get money and power — and women. What do you do?

- Invite your brother to watch more realistic movies and shows with you.
- Have a talk with your brother about fantasy and reality. Point out that, even in the shows he watches, characters who use violence often come to a bad end.
- Tell your parents about your concerns.
- Contact the people who make these programs and tell them what you like and dislike about their show's characters.

Continues . . .

6 NO BALANCE ON THE BUS

You notice that your school bus driver is polite and friendly when a girl gets on, but rude and crabby when a boy gets on. You know this is because a few of the boys are consistently obnoxious, but you feel that you are being punished for their behaviour.

- Continue to be polite to the bus driver.
- Talk with the other boys about improving their behaviour on the bus.
- Ask the girls if any of them are bothered by the difference in how students are treated on the bus.

7 Bully Blocking

A new boy in your class is being called "fag" by some bullies at your school. You know that if you try to be nice to the kid, the bullies will call you names, too.

- Make friends with the kid anyway.
- Ask your new friend how the bullying is affecting him.
- Ask your teacher if there can be class discussion about the differences between people and the seriousness of bullying.

8 MILITARY MANOEUVRES

You are in the Air Cadets. One of your best friends wants to join, but his parents are against all things they consider violent. Your friend is really angry.

- Find out why your friend wants to join the Air Cadets. Does he think the way his parents do, and the violence attracts him?
- See if your parents can talk to your friends' parents about how being an Air Cadet has been good for you.
- Invite your friend's parents to come out and see what the Air Cadets are really all about.

9 TAE KWON DO OR DON'T?

You have joined a tae kwon do club with two friends — one is a boy and one is a girl. It turns out the girl is really good, and your guy friend wants to quit because he can't let a girl be better than he is! You want all three of you to enjoy learning this together.

- Let both friends know how much you enjoy doing something together.
- If he is determined to leave the club, ask if it is really a matter of preference for him, or if it has to do with how well someone else might be doing.
- If he would really like to keep doing tae kwon do, offer to practise or attend extra classes with him so he can start feeling more confident.

10 COLUMBUS DAY

Someone posts a joke about Christopher Columbus getting lost because men never ask for directions. All the comments and responses are positive. Then someone posts a joke that says if Columbus had been a woman they would have needed six extra ships just for luggage. Now several site members are angry and the site moderator demands that the person who posted the second joke apologize or be banned from the site. You don't think this is fair.

- Post a message to the moderator pointing out the different treatment of the two people who both made stereotyping jokes.
- Try to initiate a polite discussion about why some people found the second joke offensive but not the first.
- Keep an eye out for other examples of gender discrimination in social media. You may want to speak to your parents or a school counsellor about it.

More Help

It takes time and practise to learn the skills in this book. There are many ways to deal with gender discrimination, but only you know what feels right for you in different situations. In the end, the best response is the one that prevents everyone from being hurt or treated unfairly.

If you need more information or someone to talk to, these resources might help.

Helplines

Kids Help Phone 1-800-668-6868

Justice for Children and Youth 1-866-999-JCFY

Web sites

Common Sense Media www.commonsensemedia.org

The Canadian Safe School Network www.canadiansafeschools.com

Kids Help Phone www.kidshelpphone.ca

Media Smarts: Men and Masculinity www.mediasmarts.ca/digital-media-literacy/media-issues/gender-representation/men-masculinity

Planned Parenthood: Gender & Gender Identity www.plannedparenthood.org/learn/sexual-orientation-gender/gender-gender-identity

Books

The Best Man by Richard Peck. Penguin, 2016.

Hardball by Steven Barwin. Orca, 2014.

Tap Out by Sean Rodman. Orca, 2015.

Beautiful Music for Ugly Children by Christin Cronn-Mills. Flux, 2012.

The Boy's Body Book, Everything You Need to Know About Growing Up You by Kelli Dunham. Applesauce Press, 2007, 3rd edition.

American Medical Association Boy's Guide to Becoming a Teen. Jossey-Bass, 2006.

Find other titles in the Deal With It series at www.lorimer.ca/dealwithit

Additional © illustrations on pages:

1 – Ben Shannon

4 – boy showing bicep: Ben Shannon; smartphone: Ben Shannon; hockey players: Dan Workman

5 – guitar: Jeremy Tankard; with crying girl: Remie Geoffroi; wheelchair: Ben Shannon

8 – baseball girl: Nick Johnson

9 – arm-in-arm: Dan Workman

10 – Remie Geoffroi

11 – boy holding elbow: Geraldine Charette

13 – birth certificate: Nick Johnson

14 – Ben Shannon

15 - high-five: Brooke Kerrigan

18 - talking: Jeremy Tankard

21 – arms crossed: Dan Workman; skateboard: Brooke Kerrigan; electric guitar: Nick Johnson

24 – Brooke Kerrigan

26 – Ben Shannon

27 – boy and man talking: Brooke Kerrigan; boys talking & boy in wheelchair: Remie Geoffroi

29 – basketball: Nick Johnson; gangs on TV: Bjoern Arthurs

Text copyright © 2005, 2017 by Steve Pitt

Illustrations copyright © 2005, 2017 by Steven Murray

James Lorimer & Company Ltd., Publishers acknowledges the support of the Ontario Arts Council (OAC), an agency of the Government of Ontario. We acknowledge the support of the Canada Council for the Arts, which last year invested $153 million to bring the arts to Canadians throughout the country. This project has been made possible in part by the Government of Canada and with the support of the Ontario Media Development Corporation.

Design: Blair Kerrigan/Glyphics

Cover image: iStock

Library and Archives Canada Cataloguing in Publication

Pitt, Steve, 1954-, author
  Guyness : deal with it body and soul / by Steve Pitt ; illustrated by Steven Murray. -- [New edition]

(Deal with it)
Includes bibliographical references.
ISBN 978-1-4594-1187-6 (hardback)

  1. Boys--Psychology--Juvenile literature. 2. Masculinity-- Juvenile literature. 3. Gender identity-- Juvenile literature.
I. Murray, Steven, illustrator II. Title. III. Series: Deal with it (Toronto, Ont.)

HQ799.6.P58 2017   j155.3'32   C2016-906889-7

James Lorimer & Company Ltd., Publishers
117 Peter Street, Suite 304
Toronto, ON, Canada
M5V 0M3
www.lorimer.ca

American edition published in 2017
Distributed by: Lerner Publishing Group
1251 Washington Ave N
Minneapolis, MN, USA
55401

Printed and bound in Hong Kong.